Beautiful
Beaded Gifts

Irène Lassus and Marie-Anne Voituriez

David and Charles

ACKNOWLEDGMENTS

TOUT À LOISIRS
50, rue des Archives
75004 Paris
Tel.: 01 48 87 08 87

LOISIRS ET CRÉATIONS
53, rue de Passy
75016 Paris
Tel.: 01 42 15 13 43
A list of addresses for Loisirs et Créations' 12 sales outlets
can be obtained by calling 01 41 80 64 00

ENTRÉE DES FOURNISSEURS
8, rue des Francs-Bourgeois
75003 Paris
Tel.: 01 48 87 58 98

A DAVID & CHARLES BOOK
David & Charles is a subsidiary of F+W (UK) Ltd.,
an F+W Publications Inc. company

First published in the UK in 2005
Originally published as *Miniatures de perles* by Dessain et Tolra, France 2003

Copyright © Dessain et Tolra / Larousse, Paris 2005

Distributed in North America
by F+W Publications, Inc.
4700 East Galbraith Road
Cincinnati, OH 45236
1-800-289-0963

A catalogue record for this book is available from the British Library.

ISBN 0 7153 2036 X

Printed in Singapore   by KHL Printing Co Pte Ltd
for David & Charles
Brunel House   Newton Abbot   Devon

Visit our website at www.davidandcharles.co.uk

David & Charles books are available from all good bookshops; alternatively you can contact our
Orderline on (0)1626 334555 or write to us at FREEPOST EX2 110, David & Charles Direct,
Newton Abbot, TQ12 4ZZ (no stamp required UK mainland).

Contents

*Key to
symbols*

Easy

*Of moderate
difficulty*

Complicated

Inexpensive

Reasonable

Fairly expensive

*The cost of each project is given beside the list of materials required on the pages indicated above.
These figures take into account the cost of support materials such as canvas or felt.*

Introduction

Miniature objects made from beads can be decorative, sophisticated or simply out of the ordinary. Bead miniatures take no time at all to make and use very few materials: wire and beads and a little fabric are all you need to make most of these beautiful designs.

A range of simple but fun techniques are used to create these clever miniatures. Try your hand at embroidery, canvas work and threading. The projects have been carefully selected to appeal to all tastes and standards. Combining beads with other materials such as fabrics, card and wire means that you can create a wide range of decorative designs. There are delicate candleholders, eye-catching display windows, toys and festive decorations. They are fun to make and will brighten up your own home or make thoughtful presents for people of all ages to enjoy.

FABRIC GLUE

WIRE CUTTERS

FLAT-NOSED PLIERS

NEEDLES

Basic Equipment

JEWELLERY GLUE: used to secure beads. The final bead on a length of wire is often secured with a little glue.

FABRIC GLUE: for gluing on ribbons and braid and sticking pieces of fabric together. This glue is invisible when dry.

WIRE CUTTERS: can cut through any thickness of wire with ease.

FLAT-NOSED PLIERS: used to shape wire and crush crimp beads.

NEEDLES: choose the needle according to the size of hole in the bead. Long, fine needles are best suited to beadwork.

FOAM BOARD: an excellent material that is easy to cut, glue, sand down and paint.

EMBROIDERY THREADS/SILKS: made up of six strands which can be easily separated according to the thickness of the embroidery work to be done. Embroidery threads come in a wide range of colours and have an incredible sheen.

MEDIUM WIRE

ENAMELLED WIRE

Wire

Wire comes in a variety of widths. In this book three widths are used:

THIN WIRE: for linking sections and threading beads.

MEDIUM WIRE: a firmer wire for shaping objects.

THICK WIRE: used to add a certain solidity to structures.

ENAMELLED WIRE: comes in a variety of colours, and is a strong wire that does not kink.

LAMPSHADE RINGS: metal rings that come in a range of diameters. They can be purchased from specialist home improvement stores.

THIN WIRE

Fabrics

FELT: is easy to work with; its greatest attribute is that it does not fray. It comes in lots of different colours and is a great support material for beadwork.

IRON-ON FABRIC: adheres to fabric with heat. It stiffens and prevents frayed edges when cut.

FOAM SHEET: thin foam sheets that come in a variety of colours and are easy to cut.

MEDIUM DOUBLE CANVAS: also known as Penelope. This is a common tapestry canvas and is suitable for embroidery with beads. Match the gauge of the canvas to the size of the bead: a medium or fine gauge is usually best.

SILK: the shiny lustre of silk makes it the perfect fabric to use with beads and sequins.

ORGANDIE: a starched cotton netting that comes in many different colours.

SILK

FELT

ORGANDIE

Beads and Sequins

SMALL CLEAR GLASS BEADS: are usually round, but can also be a more oval shape. Opaque or transparent, they come in a variety of colours including gold and silver.

FACETED BEADS: come in different sizes and in a wide range of colours in plastic or glass. They create interesting effects by reflecting the light. When making candle holders or creations involving candles, use glass beads which do not melt.

SEQUINS: sequins come in flat and faceted versions with centre or side perforations and may be opaque, shiny or iridescent. They are ideal for making scale effects. They can be sewn on to fabric or threaded on with beads. They also come in stars, hearts, flowers and many other shapes.

ROUND BEADS: are frequently combined with small glass beads to create attractive designs.

BUGLES: are long beads that come in all colours and can be opaque or transparent. They are often used as flower stems or for fringing.

CRIMP BEADS: small metal beads used to secure beads when knotting is impractical or for joining wires together, spacing beads or finishing rows. They are crushed with flat-nosed pliers to secure.

WOODEN BEADS: are often painted and glossy. Matt beads are easy to decorate with felt-tip pens.

STUDS OR CABOCHONS: come in a variety of colours, in glass or plastic. They can be sewn or glued on to fabrics.

STITCHED SEQUINS: are sold by the metre and come pre-stitched together.

Embroidered Photo Frame

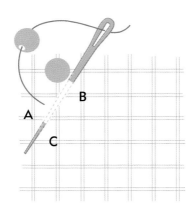

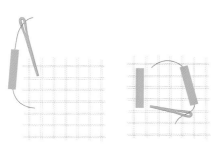

MATERIALS REQUIRED

- *small beads in silver*
- *bugles in pink and mauve*
- *a fine needle*
- *white thread*
- *medium double canvas*
- *white card*
- *gel glue*
- *small pointed scissors*

> Ensure that the size of your beads matches the gauge of your canvas.

1. Sew on the silver beads (follow the grid on page 59). Bring the threaded needle out at A, thread on a bead then go back through at B and come up again at C. Repeat this process as you work from top to bottom. When starting off, leave a length of thread on the reverse of the fabric and stitch the first few stitches over it. At the end of the row, turn the canvas and continue.

2. Next, sew on the bugles. Bring the threaded needle up through a hole in the canvas, thread on a bead then take the needle back through the canvas so that the bugle lies flat. Come up through the next hole, thread on another bead and go back through the canvas so the bead lies flat. Continue laying the beads out alongside each other until the pattern is complete (follow the grid on page 59).

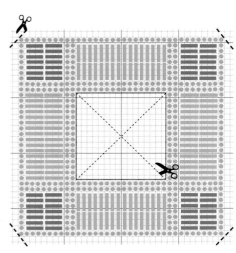

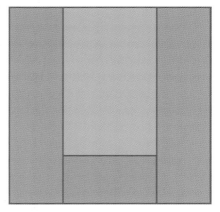

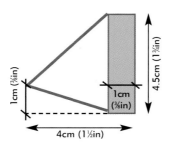

3. Trim the canvas 1.5cm (⅝in) from the edge of the beads. Cut the corners on the diagonal. Cut a window in the centre 1.5cm (⅝in) from the beads. Fold the canvas to the back and glue down. Trim any excess threads.

4. Cut out a piece of card the same size as the embroidered frame to make the backing. Cut three strips of card slightly narrower than the sides of the embroidered frame. Glue two of the strips vertically and one strip horizontally to the backing board, so that you can insert a photograph or picture. Glue the embroidered frame to the three strips of card.

5. To make a stand, cut a 4.5 x 4cm (1¾ x 1½in) rectangle from the card. Score a vertical line 1cm (⅜in) from the right edge. Cut the left-hand section into a triangle following the measurements shown above. Glue the vertical strip to the centre of the frame backing, positioning it towards its base. Fold the triangle back along the scored line.

MATERIALS REQUIRED

3-COLOURED FRAME

- *small beads in mauve, yellow and green*
- *a fine needle*
- *white thread*
- *medium double canvas*
- *white card*
- *gel glue*
- *small pointed scissors*

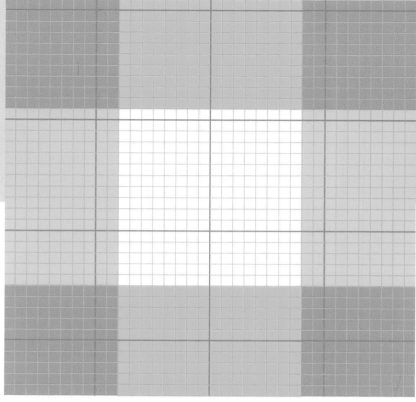

Sew the beads on to the canvas (see page 8, step 1). Follow the grid above for the 3-Coloured Frame and above right for the Pink and Orange Frame. Make up frame and stand to complete (see page 8, steps 3–5).

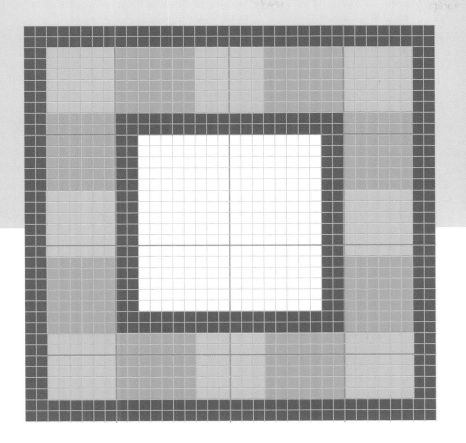

MATERIALS REQUIRED
PINK AND ORANGE FRAME
- *small glass beads in pink, red, pale orange and dark orange*
- *a fine needle*
- *white thread*
- *medium double canvas*
- *white card*
- *gel glue*
- *small pointed scissors*

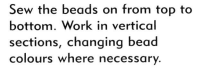

Sew the beads on from top to bottom. Work in vertical sections, changing bead colours where necessary.

Miniature Garden

MATERIALS REQUIRED

APPLE TREE

- enamelled wire in brown
- medium wire
- thin wire
- wire cutters
- small glass beads in brown, deep red, green and pale green
- medium-sized faceted beads in red

FLOWERS

- thin wire
- wire cutters
- small glass beads in white, orange, pale green and green
- gold sequins

APPLE TREE

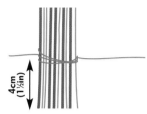

1 Use the wire cutters to cut five 25cm (10in) lengths of brown enamelled wire and five 25cm (10in) lengths of medium wire. Bunch them together and tie a 50cm (20in) length of thin wire 4cm (1½in) from the bottom.

2 Thread brown and deep red beads on to the thin wire. Wind these beads around the bunched wires working upwards for 6cm (2⅜in). Finish the trunk by twisting the wire around just above the last few beads.

3 To make a branch, twist one length of brown wire around a length of medium wire. Make the leaves as you work, making roughly six leaves per branch.

4 To make the leaves, thread six green and pale green beads on to the brown wire. Bend the wire to create a small loop. Thread twelve more green beads on to the wire and bend the wire to make another loop around the first loop.

5 Between the leaves, thread a red faceted bead on to the brown wire and twist the wire around to secure each apple. Each branch should have around four apples. Trim the excess wire at the end of each branch.

FLOWERS

1 Take a 50cm (20in) length of thin wire and thread eight white beads on it. Slide them into the centre of the wire. Make a small loop of beads and twist the wire to secure. Thread on another eight beads, loop and twist next to the previous twist. Repeat to make six petals.

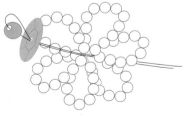

2 Bring the six petals together by twisting the wire then threading on a gold sequin and an orange bead and take the wire back through the sequin to form the centre of the flower.

3 Thread five green beads on to the two lengths of wire at the same time to make the stalk. Make a leaf (see Apple Tree, step 4). Finish off the stalk by threading on four green beads. Trim the excess wire 4cm (1½in) from the last green bead.

MATERIALS REQUIRED

BASKET
- *medium wire*
- *thin wire*
- *wire cutters*
- *small glass beads in orange*
- *jewellery glue*

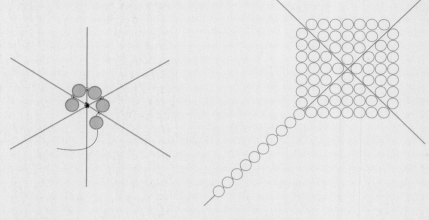

BASKET

CHAIR

CHAIR
- *medium wire*
- *thin wire*
- *wire cutters*
- *small glass beads in turquoise green*
- *jewellery glue*

BASKET

1 Cut three 20cm (8in) lengths of medium wire and a 1m (39in) length of thin wire. Lay the three lengths of wire out in a star shape and bind them at the centre with one end of the thin wire.

2 Thread an orange bead on to the thin wire and wind it around one of the spokes of medium wire. Thread on another bead and wind the thin wire around the next spoke. Repeat this process around all the wires, with each bead sitting between the points of the star. On the second loop, thread on two beads between each point of the star. Repeat this process until you are threading on five beads at once. Make six loops with five beads, then pull up the ends of wire to make the basket.

3 Thread 22 beads on to one of the lengths of medium wire to form the handle. Bend the wire over and secure it with a little glue to the opposite side of the basket. Trim the excess lengths of medium wire and wind their ends around the thin wire at the top of the basket.

CHAIR

1 Cut two 30cm (12in) lengths of medium wire. Position them in a cross shape and bind them at the centre with one end of a 30cm (12in) length of thin wire.

2 Use the same technique as for the basket. Thread a turquoise green bead on to the thin wire and wind the wire around one of the spokes of medium wire. Thread on one bead between each spoke of medium wire on the first loop, three on the second, five on the third and seven on the fourth. Thread ten beads on to each end of medium wire to make the chair legs. Secure the final bead on each leg with a little glue. Bend the legs down.

3 Cut an 8cm (3⅛in) length of medium wire to make the back of the chair. Thread on turquoise green beads and twist the wire to make the chair back. Use the excess wire to secure the back to the back legs of the chair.

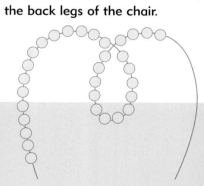

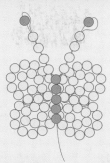

BUTTERFLY

1 Cut two 20cm (8in) lengths of thin wire and make up two sets of two wings in the same way as the Apple Tree leaves (see page 12, step 4). Each wing is made up of one small loop with seven beads and one large loop with sixteen beads. Leave wire to secure to body.

2 Cut a 14cm (5½in) length of thin wire. Thread a blue bead to the centre. Loop an end of wire over it and thread four beads over both wires. Thread four sky blue beads and one blue bead on to each antenna (see above). Do not trim excess wire.

HOW TO MAKE UP THE DISPLAY WINDOW

1 Cut a rectangle of green felt to fit into the base of the box. Embroider some blades of grass and poppies on the felt. To make the grass, thread a needle with some green thread and push it through the felt. Thread on three or four pale green bugles and a small glass bead in green. Pass the thread around the last bead and go back through all the other beads. Go back into the felt and tie a knot on the reverse. To make the poppies, work in the same way using three pale green bugles, one red sequin and one black bead.

2 Push the flowers and the tree through the felt. Secure them on the reverse with a little glue and some tape.

3 Paint the outside and edges of the box in sky blue. Measure the inside of the box (back, sides and top) and cut a piece of sky blue cotton to fit. Sew a few white sequins on the sky blue fabric (see diagram below).

4 Attach the butterfly to the sky blue fabric, pushing the wire through the fabric and bending it back on the reverse. Secure with some tape. Leave roughly 4cm (1½in) wire between the fabric and the butterfly's body.

5 Apply a layer of glue to the back, top and sides of the box and position the sky blue fabric inside. Glue the felt floor to the base of the box and stitched sequins to the edges; use green sequins along the bottom and sky blue sequins on the top and sides.

MATERIALS REQUIRED

BUTTERFLY
- *thin wire*
- *small glass beads in blue and sky blue*
- *wire cutters*

DISPLAY WINDOW
- *small rectangular box 14 × 19cm (5½ × 7½in)*
- *green felt*
- *green thread*
- *a fine needle*
- *bugles in pale green*
- *small glass beads in pale green, green and black*
- *sequins in red and white*
- *adhesive tape*
- *fabric glue*
- *acrylic paint in sky blue*
- *paintbrush*
- *stitched sequins in sky blue and green*
- *sky blue cotton fabric*
- *wire cutters*

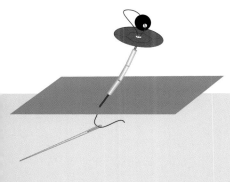

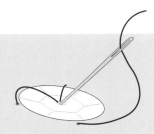

Butterfly Tumblers

MATERIALS REQUIRED

To make one butterfly

- *medium wire*
- *wire cutters*
- *flat-nosed pliers*
- *thin wire*
- *small glass beads in pink*
- *2 faceted beads in pink*
- *jewellery glue*
- *suction pad*

1 To make up the frame for the butterfly, cut a 60cm (24in) length of medium wire. Bend and shape the wire to make a butterfly (see template, page 59), working from point A to B. Use flat-nosed pliers to make neat points in the wings. Twist the wire at the base of the antennae to secure.

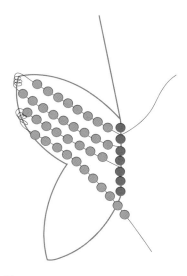

3 To make up the inside of the wings, cut an 80cm (31½in) length of thin wire. Find its middle point and secure it at the top of the butterfly's body (at the base of the antennae). Thread as many beads as necessary on to the wire to reach the edge of the wing. Wind the wire three times around the edge of the wing and thread on more beads and secure around the butterfly's body. Repeat this process to make roughly ten rows for each wing.

4 Thread beads over 4cm (1½in) of each antenna. Finish with a faceted bead and secure with a little glue. Trim the excess wire. Attach the butterfly to a suction pad using a length of thin wire.

These pretty butterflies will brighten up any corner of your home. Stick them on bathroom or kitchen tiles, or on a window or mirror.

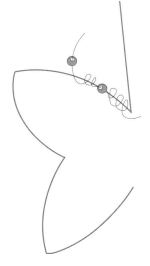

2 Cut two 60cm (24in) lengths of thin wire to decorate each wing structure. Wind the wire tightly three times around the base of the antennae and thread on a small glass bead. Wind the thin wire around twice and thread on another bead. Repeat this process all around the wing. Make up the second wing in the same way. Finish off by threading on as many beads as necessary to fill the centre of the butterfly and secure in the centre of the wings with three tight twists of the wire.

Fashion Collection**

MATERIALS REQUIRED

SCARF

- *silk in vivid pink and lime green*
- *needle and thread*
- *scissors*
- *small sequins in turquoise*
- *small glass beads in vivid pink and turquoise*

To protect these exquisite creations, keep them in a small display case painted pink or green.

SCARF

❶ **Cut a 30 x 4cm (12 x 1½in) strip of vivid pink silk and a strip of lime green silk the same size. Sew them together along one of the long edges to obtain a 30 x 7cm (12 x 2¾in) strip.**

❸ **Place the two remaining long sides right sides together and stitch. Carefully turn the scarf the right way out. Flatten out the seam. Tuck the ends inside and sew up with invisible stitching.**

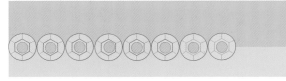

❷ **Iron open the seam and sew a row of turquoise sequins along the seam, securing each one with a pink glass bead (see page 22, step 2).**

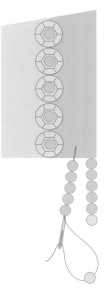

❹ **Add a fringe to each end of the scarf. Each tassel is made up of six beads – five vivid pink beads and one turquoise bead (see diagram above).**

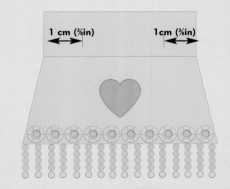

1 cm (⅜in)　　　　1cm (⅜in)

BAG

MATERIALS REQUIRED

BAG

- *silk in vivid pink and lime green*
- *scissors*
- *iron-on fabric*
- *small glass beads in vivid pink and turquoise*
- *small sequins in turquoise*
- *large heart-shaped cabochon*
- *needle and thread*
- *craft knife*
- *fabric glue*
- *press stud*

❶ Cut out a front and back for the bag from vivid green silk (see template, page 60). Next, iron a 7cm (2¾in) square of iron-on fabric to a piece of green silk and cut out the flap of the bag (see template, page 60). To make the sides and base of the bag, cut a 22 x 4cm (8¾ x 1½in) strip of vivid pink silk. To make the handle, iron a 6 x 2cm (2⅜ x ¾in) strip of iron-on fabric to the pink silk and cut out a 5 x 1cm (2 x ⅜in) strip.

❷ Stitch the sides and base strip to the front and back of the bag. Fold the ends of the sides towards the inside of the bag and mark the fold with your iron. Fold the flap along line AB, line up with the top of the back of the bag and stitch.

❸ Make a fringe along the edge of the flap. Use four small glass beads in vivid pink and one turquoise bead for each tassel. Sew on sequins along the edge securing each one with a small pink glass bead (see page 22, step 2). Sew or glue the heart-shaped cabochon to the centre of the flap. Using the craft knife, cut two small scores 1cm (⅜in) from the edges of the top to secure the pink silk handle. Thread it through and glue it down on the reverse of the flap using fabric glue. Sew a press stud to the centre back of the flap, and to the front of the bag.

MULES

① Iron a piece of iron-on fabric to the back of a piece of green silk . Cut out two mules from the backed green silk and pink felt (see template, page 60).

② Iron a piece of iron-on fabric to the back of a piece of vivid pink silk and cut two strips of vivid pink silk 2.5 x 1.5cm (1 x ⅝in). Decorate them with turquoise sequins secured with small glass beads (see page 22, step 2). Glue or sew a small heart-shaped cabochon in the centre of each strip. Insert the ends of the pink strips between the green soles and the felt soles and glue the soles together using the fabric glue.

(see template, page 60). / (see page 22, step 2).

MATERIALS REQUIRED

MULES
- *silk in vivid pink and lime green*
- *iron-on fabric*
- *pink felt*
- *turquoise sequins*
- *small glass beads*
- *2 small heart-shaped cabochons*
- *fabric glue*

CHEST OF DRAWERS
- *4 large matchboxes*
- *acrylic paint in pink and lime green*
- *paintbrush*
- *fabric glue*
- *pale pink silk*
- *iron-on fabric*
- *red wire*
- *large faceted beads in pink*
- *adhesive tape*
- *5mm (³⁄₁₆in) thick foam board*
- *superglue*
- *pins*
- *transparent sequins in pink*
- *4 large wooden beads*
- *scissors*

CHEST OF DRAWERS

① Paint four matchboxes with pink acrylic paint. Allow the boxes to dry thoroughly before gluing them together. Cut out four 5 x 3cm (2 x 1¼in) rectangles of pale pink silk. Back them with iron-on fabric and glue them to the front of the drawers. Thread a 5cm (2in) length of red wire through a large faceted bead, make a hole in the centre of the drawer front and thread the wire through. Flatten the ends out inside the drawer to fix the bead in place and secure with a short length of tape.

② Cut out two 12.5 x 8cm (5 x 3⅛in) rectangles and two 8 x 6.5cm (3⅛ x 2⅝in) rectangles from the foam board. Paint them pink and leave to dry. Glue them to the top, back and sides of the matchboxes. Use pins to secure the sequins to the foam board all around the outside edge of the chest. Paint four large wooden beads in lime green and glue them to the bottom of the chest to make the feet.

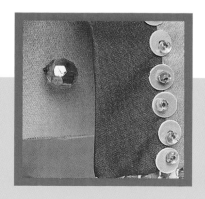

Pocket Mirror

MATERIALS REQUIRED

- *5cm (2in) square mirror*
- *2 × 8cm (3⅛in) squares of felt*
- *craft knife*
- *8 round cabochons in purple*
- *small glass beads in maroon and red*
- *a fine needle*
- *red thread*
- *small silver sequins*
- *7.5cm (3in) square of foam sheet*

The square of foam sheet helps to hold the mirror in position inside the felt frame.

① Using a craft knife, cut a 4cm (1½in) square from the centre of one of the felt squares. Sew or glue the purple cabochons to the felt frame at regular intervals. Next, sew a circle of maroon beads around each cabochon (see diagram above).

② Sew on a silver sequin between each cabochon secured by a red bead (see diagram above).

③ Using a craft knife cut out a 5cm (2in) square from the centre of the foam sheet, and place the mirror inside it. Layer the 8cm (3⅛in) felt square, foam sheet with mirror and decorated felt frame on top of each other. Sew the two felt layers together around the outside edge.

④ Hide this seam with a row of red beads (see diagram, step 1).

Evening Pochette★★

MATERIALS REQUIRED

- *12 × 20cm (4¾ × 7⅞in) black denim fabric*
- *sheet of tracing paper*
- *sheet of thin card*
- *pencil*
- *scissors*
- *white dressmaker's pencil*
- *sequins in red and black and 1 green sequin*
- *small glass beads in black*
- *enamelled wire in black*
- *black and red thread*
- *a fine needle*
- *wire cutters*
- *fabric glue*
- *reinforced tape*

Stick a piece of reinforced tape inside the pochette so that the ends of wire from the stamens won't scratch the contents of the bag.

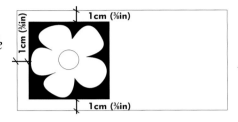

1 Trace off the flower (see template, page 60) and transfer to a piece of thin card. Cut out. Place the template on the black denim fabric and trace the outline with the dressmaker's pencil. Draw a square around the outside 1cm (⅜in) from the edge of the fabric.

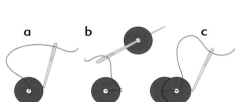

2 Start from the outside edge of the flower and sew on red sequins with red thread so that they overlap and fill the flower. Bring the needle up through the centre of the sequin (a). Take the needle back down through the fabric at the side of the sequin and bring it back up in almost the same spot (b). Thread the second sequin on the needle and position it so that it hides the hole of the first sequin (c).

3 Use the same technique at the centre of the flower, using black sequins. Finish with a green sequin secured with a black bead.

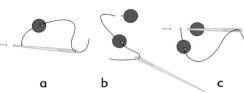

4 Fill in the square around the flower with small glass beads sewn on with black thread (see diagrams above).

5 Cut five 5cm (2in) lengths of black enamelled wire. Thread a black sequin into the centre of each length of wire and twist the two ends of wire together to make stamens. Push them through the fabric at the centre of the flower and glue them to the reverse with fabric glue.

6 Fold the fabric to make a pochette, then fold in 1cm (⅜in) along three edges and sew together with invisible stitching, starting 1cm (⅜in) from the upper edge. Make a frayed fringe from the opening to the beads.

7 Take a 1m (39in) length of strong black thread. Sew one end to one side of the pochette and thread black beads along the whole length. Secure the other end with a stitch on the opposite side of the bag.

Embroidered Love Token**

MATERIALS REQUIRED

- *2 × 10cm (4in) silk squares in vivid red and deep red*
- *iron-on fabric*
- *tracing paper and pencil*
- *white card*
- *scissors*
- *dressmaker's pencil*
- *beads in mauve, orange and yellow*
- *a fine needle*
- *red thread*
- *small glass beads in deep red*
- *pins*
- *sequins in deep red*
- *5mm (³⁄₁₆in) thick foam board*
- *superglue*
- *paintbrush*
- *red acrylic paint*
- *fine sandpaper*
- *fabric glue*
- *faceted beads in red*

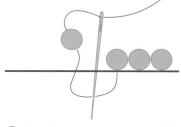

1 Iron a piece of iron-on fabric to the back of the vivid red silk square. Trace off the heart and its design (see template, page 60) and transfer to white card. Cut out. Place on the vivid red silk and draw around it with the dressmaker's pencil.

2 Outline the design inside the heart using mauve, orange and yellow beads, then fill in between the lines. Sew the beads on as indicated in the diagram above.

3 Sew small glass beads in deep red around the outside of the heart, using the same technique. Cut around the heart very close to the beads. Place the heart in the centre of the square of deep red silk and pin it to the fabric. Sew deep red sequins around the heart, secured with orange beads (see page 22, step 2).

4 Cut two 10 x 3cm (4 x 1¼in) and two 9 x 3cm (3½ x 1¼in) rectangles and one 9cm (3½in) square from the foam board. Superglue together to make a 10 x 10 x 3cm (4 x 4 x 1¼in) box with a 9cm (3½in) base. When the glue has dried, paint the box red. Sand the edges down gently with fine sandpaper and apply several coats of paint.

5 Glue the square of deep red silk with the heart to the bottom of the box with fabric glue. Pin a row of red faceted beads around the edges of the box.

Dragonfly Trinket Box

DRAGONFLY AND BOX

- *silver wire*
- *wire cutters*
- *small glass beads in pink and orange*
- *small cylindrical box with lid, 6cm (2⅜in) in diameter*
- *green felt*
- *2 small beads in pink*
- *small bugles in green*
- *small faceted beads in vivid pink*
- *a fine needle*
- *green thread*
- *fabric glue*
- *scissors*

WINGS

1 Cut a 30cm (12in) length of silver wire using your wire cutters. Thread on two orange beads and slide them into the middle of the wire.

2 Bend the wire upwards and thread three beads for the second row on to one of the ends; use the diagram shown above right as a guide to coloured beads. Cross the wires by threading the second end of wire through the three beads.

3 Thread on the next four beads and cross the wires as in the previous step.

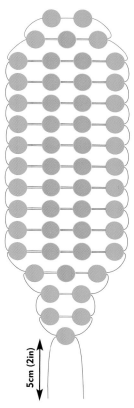

4 Continue in this way following the diagram above until all the rows are complete. Trim the excess wire 5cm (2in) from the last bead. Make up four identical wings in this way.

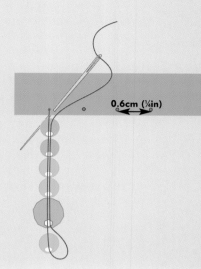

0.6cm (¼in)

DRAGONFLY BODY

5 The dragonfly's body is sewn directly on to the box. Trace the outline of the box lid on to the green felt and cut out. Draw a 4.5cm (1¾in) line down the centre of the felt circle. Sew beads on either side of the line, using the diagram left as a guide and finishing with the 2 small beads. Sew green bugles randomly over the felt circle, spacing them roughly 0.6cm (¼in) apart. Sew a row of pink beads around the edge of the felt circle.

6 Measure the width and circumference of the lid edge and cut a strip of felt to fit. Decorate with green bugles and create a fringe, spacing the tassels roughly 0.6cm (¼in) apart. Bring the needle out at the edge of the felt, thread on 2 pink, 2 orange, 1 pink faceted bead and 1 orange bead. Go around the final orange bead and take the needle back through the rest and secure in the felt.

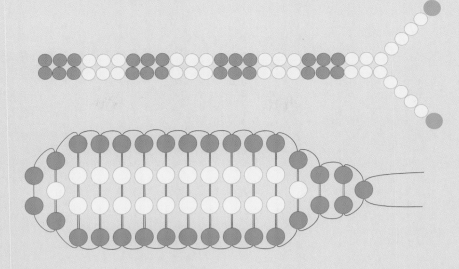

ASSEMBLING THE BOX

7 Position the wings on either side of the dragonfly body close to its head and push the wires through the felt. Twist the wires together on the reverse to secure. Using fabric glue, glue the fringed edge of the box lid and the top with the dragonfly to the top of the box. Leave to dry. Cut out a strip of felt to cover the sides of the box up to the lid and glue in place.

HAIRCLIP

You can use the same technique to create a dragonfly hairclip. Cut a piece of green felt the same size as the hairclip mount. Draw a line down the centre and sew beads either side of the line to make the dragonfly's body. Follow the diagram above as a guide. Make the wings following the diagram above as a guide to the number and colour of the beads required (also see page 28, steps 1–4). Make up four identical wings. Push the wires of the wings through the felt and twist on the reverse to secure. Glue the felt with the dragonfly to the hairclip mount.

MATERIALS REQUIRED

HAIRCLIP

- *hairclip mount*
- *green felt*
- *fabric glue and scissors*
- *small glass beads in dark orange and pearlized pink*
- *needle and thread*
- *2 small pink beads*
- *silver wire*

Why not use the same technique to make a brooch? Simply glue the felt with your dragonfly to a brooch mount. Adapt the dimensions to fit the mount if necessary.

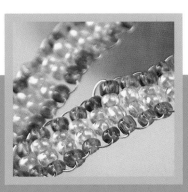

Scented Pouch *

MATERIALS REQUIRED

- *organdie in mauve and white*
- *tracing paper and pencil*
- *white paper*
- *dressmaker's pencil*
- *fabric paint in pale mauve and purple*
- *paintbrush*
- *small embroidery beads in silver*
- *mauve sequins*
- *fine beading needle*
- *pale mauve thread*

You could vary the colour of organdie according to the fragrance you have chosen.

① Cut a 10cm (4in) square and two rectangles 7 x 10cm (2¾ x 4in) from the mauve organdie. Trace off the ribbon template (see page 61) and transfer to a sheet of white paper. Place the organdie square over the template and trace it on to the fabric with the dressmaker's pencil. Paint the inside of the bow purple and the rest in mauve. Remove the fabric from the paper and allow to dry.

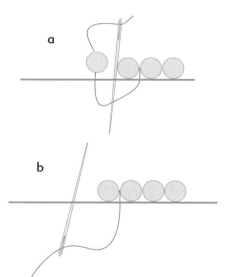

a

b

② Sew silver beads around the outline of the ribbon motif using the technique shown above (steps a and b). Outline the folds in the bow in the same way. Sew a scattering of mauve sequins around the bow, securing each with a small bead (see page 22, step 2).

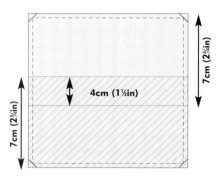

7cm (2¾in)

4cm (1½in)

7cm (2¾in)

③ Turn under and stitch along one long edge of each organdie rectangle to neaten. Place the rectangles right sides together with the embroidered square, overlapping the neatened edges of the rectangles as shown in the diagram above. Stitch around the outside of the pouch, trim the corners diagonally and turn the pouch the right way out. Press carefully.

④ Cut two 10cm (4in) squares from white organdie. Place right sides together and stitch around the outside, leaving a small opening to put your lavender in. Stitch up the opening with invisible stitching. Place the lavender sachet inside the embroidered pouch.

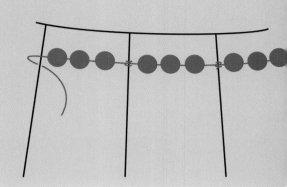

MATERIALS REQUIRED

PURPLE LAMPSHADE

- *medium silver wire*
- *thin silver wire*
- *small faceted glass beads in orange, red, purple and pink*

1 Make the lampshade frame and decorate the rings and side wires (see page 36, steps 1–3).

2 Cut five 20cm (8in) lengths of thin wire. Attach one end to a side wire with three tight turns between two beads. Thread on as many beads as necessary, alternating colours as you work, and wind the wire around the next side wire. Continue in this way until you reach your starting point again. Fill in the lampshade with five horizontal rows.

MATERIALS REQUIRED

RED LAMPSHADE

- *medium silver wire*
- *small faceted glass beads in maroon, vivid red and pink*
- *thin silver wire*
- *enamelled wire in red*
- *red sequins*

RED LAMPSHADE

1 Make the lampshade frame and decorate the rings and side wires (see page 36, steps 1–3).

2 Cut a 1.5m (4ft 11in) length of red enamelled wire. Attach the wire to a side wire between two beads, with three tight turns. Thread on a sequin, then wind the wire around the next side wire. Continue in this way until you reach your starting point then continue to the bottom of the frame.

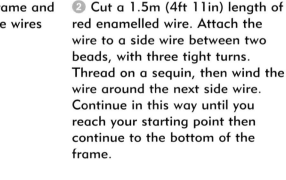

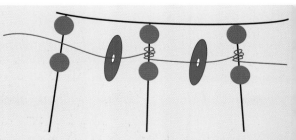

LAMPSHADE BASE

① Cut an 8cm (3⅛in) and a 5.5cm (2⅛in) diameter circle from the foam board. Hollow out a small circle with the end of the pencil in the centre of each of the circles. Paint the two circles of foam board and the metal part of the tea light. Choose a colour that matches the beads on the shade.

② Cut a 7.5cm (3in) length of pencil. Wind enamelled wire tightly over the length of the pencil. Secure the wire with a little glue at both ends. Place each end of the pencil into one of the foam board circles.

③ Glue sequins side by side around the edge of the smaller bottom circle and the upper circle. Glue the metal part of the tea light to the centre of the large circle. Balance the shade on top of the larger foam circle.

MATERIALS REQUIRED

LAMPSHADE BASE

- *5mm (³⁄₁₆in) thick foam board*
- *pair of compasses*
- *rounded pencil*
- *acrylic paint to match*
- *paintbrush*
- *enamelled wire*
- *faceted sequins*
- *tea light candle*
- *scissors*
- *superglue*

Flower Lights**

MATERIALS REQUIRED

To make one flower

- *thin wire*
- *wire cutters*
- *small glass beads in pale orange, dark orange and red*
- *5 faceted beads in pale orange, dark orange and red*
- *battery-powered lights*

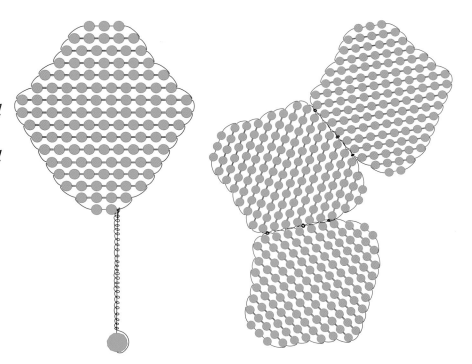

These flowers make a stunning table centrepiece for any special occasion.

❶ To make one petal cut a 60cm (24in) length of thin wire. Thread 3 glass beads into the middle of the wire. Bend the wire upwards and thread 5 pale orange beads on one end of wire and cross the wires by taking the second end of wire through these beads (see page 28, steps 1–4). Continue rows in this order: 6 beads, 7, 9, 10, 12, 12, 11, 10, 9, 8, 7, 6, 4 and 2 beads. Thread a matching faceted bead on to the remaining length of wire at the base of the petal. Bend the wire back and wind it around itself as shown in the diagram above to make the pistil. Make up five petals in this way.

❷ Cut small pieces of wire to link the outsides of the petals together. When you have joined the five petals together, thread some wire through the ten beads in the centre and pull to bring the petals together. Push some small bulbs up through each of the flowers and secure them by winding wire around them. Make up two more five-petalled flowers using the dark orange and red small glass beads.

Festive Table Settings

MATERIALS REQUIRED

CHERRIES

- *4 wooden beads 2cm (¾in) in diameter with 4mm (⅙in) holes*
- *a fine needle*
- *strong red thread*
- *small glass beads in cherry red, coral pink, dark green and pale green*
- *thin wire*
- *wire cutters*
- *jewellery glue*

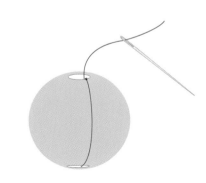

① Push the needle, threaded with red thread, through and around one of the large wooden beads and tie a knot.

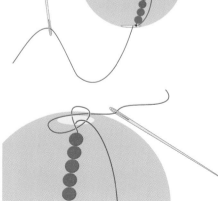

② Thread on small cherry red glass beads, and before entering the hole in the bead, secure to the previous row with a small blanket stitch. Depending on the size of the small glass beads, alternate the rows between thirteen and fifteen beads or fourteen and sixteen beads. Alternating will allow you to maintain the shape of the round wooden bead. Make up two cherry red cherries and two coral pink cherries.

③ Cut a 40cm (15½in) length of thin wire and halve it. To make up the leaves, use the same technique as for the Dragonfly Box (see page 28, steps 1–4). Thread on pale green beads as follows: for the large leaves, 2 beads, 3 beads, 4 beads, 5, 6, 7, 9, 9, 9, 8, 7, 6, 5, 3 and 2 beads. For the small leaves: 2 beads, 3 beads, 4 beads, 5, 6, 7, 7, 7, 6, 5, 4, 3 and 2 beads. Repeat this process using the dark green beads.

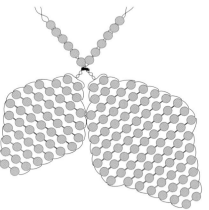

④ At the end of each leaf, twist the remaining length of wire together and thread on green beads over roughly 4cm (1½in). Bend the excess wire back on itself and twist it to prevent the beads from falling off. Join a small and a large leaf by twisting them together at their base. Thread the beaded stalks into the cherries and secure them with a little glue.

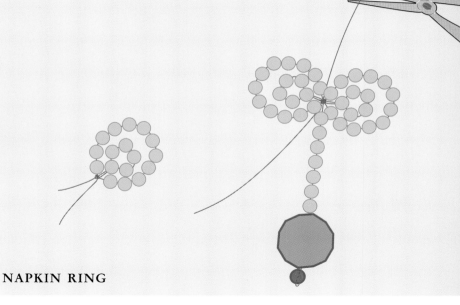

NAPKIN RING

MATERIALS REQUIRED

NAPKIN RING

- *medium red wire*
- *thin wire*
- *wire cutters*
- *small glass beads in cherry red and pale green*
- *4 faceted beads in cherry red*
- *flat-nosed pliers*

❶ Using wire cutters, cut a 60cm (24in) length of red wire and a 1m (39in) length of thin wire. Start by making up the leaves and the cherries. Thread five pale green beads 15cm (6in) from the end of the thin wire. Twist the beaded wire to make a loop. Thread on twelve pale green beads and bend the wire so that it fits around the first circle. Repeat this process to make a second leaf adjacent to the first.

❷ Thread seven pale green beads on to one end of wire then thread on one red faceted bead and one small red bead. Go over the red bead and back through all the beads in the stalk. Grip the wire between the flat-nosed pliers, wind it twice around the leaves and make up the second stalk and the second cherry, repeating the process as before. Trim any excess wire.

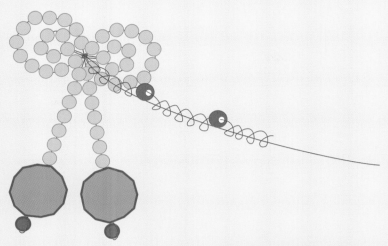

CANDLEHOLDER

3 Bend the end of the red wire 1cm (⅜in) back on itself, and secure to the cherry leaves. Wind thin wire around the red wire and thread on a red bead at roughly 1cm (⅜in) intervals.

4 At the end of the red wire, make up a cherry using the same process as before (steps 1 and 2). Wrap the ring around your napkin.

To make the candleholder, follow the instructions for the Napkin Ring. Place several cherries along the length of the wire, alternating the colours as follows: red, pink, orange, red, orange, pink. Alternate between coral pink beads and cherry red beads as you twist the thin wire around the red wire. Make up red cherries with dark green leaves, and pink and orange cherries with pale green leaves. The length of the red wire depends on the circumference of the candleholder. Place the final cherry 5cm (2in) from the end and finish with a loop of beads. These will be used for fastening the wire around the first cherry and securing to the candleholder.

MATERIALS REQUIRED

CANDLEHOLDER
- *medium red wire*
- *thin wire*
- *wire cutters*
- *small glass beads in cherry red, coral pink, pale green and dark green*
- *4 faceted beads in cherry red*
- *4 faceted beads in vivid pink*
- *4 faceted beads in orange*

Doll Pendants

MATERIALS REQUIRED

Brunette doll

- *thin wire*
- *silver wire*
- *wire cutters*
- *flat sequins in turquoise*
- *crimp beads*
- *1 large wooden bead*
- *2 medium-sized wooden beads in orange*
- *opaque small glass beads in blue, black, red and green*
- *medium-sized vivid pink beads*
- *vermilion red felt*
- *long beads*
- *multicoloured sequins*
- *red heart-shaped cabochon*
- *fine needle*
- *red thread*
- *flat-nosed pliers*
- *jewellery glue*
- *scissors*

1 Cut a 35cm (13½in) length of silver wire. Double it, taking care not to flatten the loop. Thread a crimp bead, a sequin and the large wooden bead up to the loop. To make the doll's hair, cut 8 x 8cm (3⅛in) lengths of thin wire. Thread on a coloured small glass bead, bend the wire back over the bead and secure with a twist. Thread on 3cm (1¼in) of black beads. Repeat seven more times.

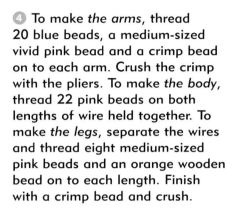

2 Apply a little glue to the eight strands of hair and place them inside the wooden bead, around the silver wire. Cover the hole in the wooden bead with the sequin and crush the crimp bead using the pliers.

3 Thread a turquoise sequin, two green beads and a crimp bead on to the two ends of wire below the wooden bead. Thread 10cm (4in) wire through the crimp bead to form the arms and crush the bead.

4 To make *the arms*, thread 20 blue beads, a medium-sized vivid pink bead and a crimp bead on to each arm. Crush the crimp with the pliers. To make *the body*, thread 22 pink beads on both lengths of wire held together. To make *the legs*, separate the wires and thread eight medium-sized pink beads and an orange wooden bead on to each length. Finish with a crimp bead and crush.

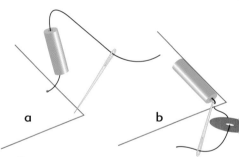

a   b

5 Cut the doll's dress out of felt (see template, page 61). Decorate the bottom of the dress with a fringe made with long beads and sequins (see diagram above).

6 Sew or glue the heart-shaped cabochon to the centre front of the dress. Wrap the dress around the doll, passing it through the slit at the back. Secure the dress by sewing two beads on the slit at the back and under the arms to secure the sides.

Christmas Decorations ⋆⋆

MATERIALS REQUIRED

MISTLETOE WREATH

- *thin wire*
- *wire cutters*
- *small bugles in green*
- *large round pearlized beads*
- *small glass pearlized beads*
- *lampshade ring, 10cm (4in) in diameter*
- *jewellery glue*
- *transparent ribbon, 1cm (⅜in) wide*

🌙 Why not match the colour of your beads to your other Christmas decorations?

1 To make the strands of mistletoe, use wire cutters to cut a 50cm (20in) length of thin wire. Thread on 3cm (1¼in) of small green bugles and slide them into the centre of the wire. Next, bend this length of wire in half and make a little twist. Do not trim the excess wire.

2 Thread on enough green bugles to go around the first loop. Twist the wire around itself. Flatten the two concentric oval shapes to make a leaf.

3 Make up a second leaf in the same way then make the berries. Thread three green bugles, one large round pearlized bead and one small glass pearlized bead on to one of the ends. Take the wire back over the small pearlized bead and back through the other beads. Twist the wire between the leaves to secure. Make up three mistletoe berries.

4 Make up fifteen leaves with berries to form the wreath. Twist their wire ends around the lampshade ring to attach, spreading them evenly around the circle. Apply a little glue to the back of the ring to hold the leaves in place. To finish, tie a small bow of transparent tape at the top of the wreath.

Beaded Bird Mobile

MATERIALS REQUIRED

- *1 lampshade ring, 15cm (5⅞in) in diameter*
- *felt in pink, orange, red, purple, turquoise and green*
- *thin wire*
- *wire cutters*
- *bugles in pink, orange and turquoise*
- *small glass beads in vivid pink, dark pink, deep red, fuchsia, purple, turquoise, opaque green, iridescent green and orange*
- *superglue*
- *embroidery thread in lavender, Christmas red, Nile green and bright turquoise*
- *needle*
- *star-shaped cabochons in pink, turquoise and red*
- *round cabochons in pink, turquoise and red*
- *scissors*

PINK BIRD

1 Cut out two bird shapes from pink felt and two wing shapes from purple felt (see template, page 61). Ensure you have a right side and wrong side for each.

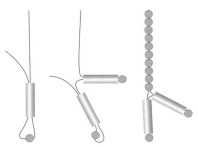

2 To make the feet, take two 12cm (4¾in) lengths of thin wire. Thread on a pink bugle and a pink bead and go back through the bugle. Thread on a second bugle and a bead and go back through the bugle. Finish with 10 pink beads (see diagram above). Make up two feet. Make the tail using the same technique, with three pink bugles and three pink beads.

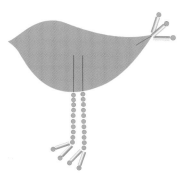

3 Glue the feet and tail to the wrong side of the bird's body and glue the two bird's bodies together.

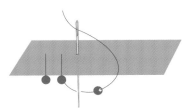

4 Sew the two halves of the bird together with a blanket stitch. Use two strands of the lavender embroidery thread and thread on a pink bead with each stitch. Place the stitches quite close together.

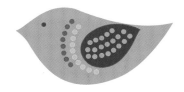

5 Embroider the wings with fuchsia, dark pink and pink beads as shown in the diagram above and superglue to the bird's body. Decorate the body with beads as shown then sew on the eye.

Make up two more birds in the same way. To make the turquoise and green bird, use turquoise, opaque green and iridescent green beads, and green thread. To make the purple and orange bird, use orange, deep red and purple beads, and red thread.

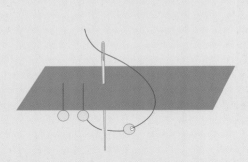

CLOUDS

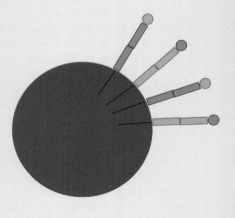

SUN

1 Cut two clouds from pink felt (see template, page 61). Decide on a right and a wrong side for each. Sew or glue three turquoise cabochons to each half. Glue the two halves of the cloud wrong sides together. Edge with blanket stitch using two strands of lavender embroidery thread and threading on a pink bead with each stitch.

2 Make up a turquoise cloud using the same technique. Sew or glue pink cabochons to the turquoise cloud and edge with green blanket stitch with turquoise beads. Sew or glue red cabochons to a purple cloud, and edge with red blanket stitch, threading on an orange bead with every stitch.

1 Cut two 4cm (1½in) diameter circles from red felt. Sew or glue a star-shaped turquoise cabochon in the centre of each. To make the sun's rays, cut 38 x 5cm (2in) lengths of thin wire. Thread two orange bugles and a turquoise bead on to half the lengths of wire and two turquoise bugles and one orange bead on to the other. Take the wire around the bead and back through the bugles. Glue the rays around the sun, alternating the colours as you go, and then glue the two halves of the sun together. Leave to dry.

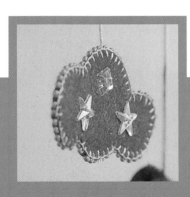

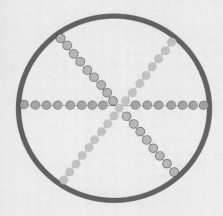

MOBILE FRAME

① Attach one end of a length of thin wire to the lampshade ring by winding it around the ring. Thread on some orange beads, then attach the wire at the opposite point on the ring. Make two further cross rows in this way, one with green beads and one with pink.

② Wrap turquoise embroidery thread around the ring. Hang the birds and clouds from cotton threads of varying lengths. Attach each bird or cloud to the ring at the end of a beaded cross row. Alternate between birds and clouds and attach a length of the same coloured thread each time for hanging the mobile up. Hang the sun from the centre, at the point where the three cross rows intersect. Bring all the threads together and hang the mobile.

Miniature Candle Chandelier

MATERIALS REQUIRED

- *medium wire*
- *thin enamelled wire in purple*
- *wire cutters*
- *small faceted glass beads in purple and red*
- *small glass beads in pink*
- *large faceted glass beads in pink*
- *jewellery glue*

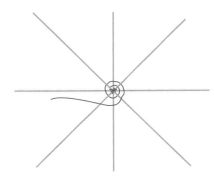

1 Using wire cutters, cut three 30cm (12in) lengths of medium wire and roughly 2m (6ft 7in) of thin wire. Lay the three lengths of medium wire on top of each other at their central points and bind them with four tight turns of one end of the thin wire. Spread out the branches of medium wire so that they are equidistant.

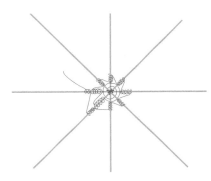

2 To make the base of the chandelier, wind the thin wire four times around one of the branches and move to the next branch. Repeat this process to make eight loops around the branches.

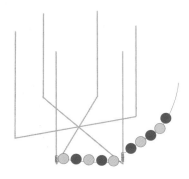

3 Bend the six branches upwards and thread on five faceted glass beads before moving to the next branch. Alternate the colours as you go. Wind the thin wire around each branch six times before moving to the next branch. Make up seven rows of beads in this way.

4 Using wire cutters trim the lengths of the six branches of the frame to 7.5cm (3in) above the last row of beads. Next, for each of the six branches, cut a 40cm (16in) length of thin purple wire, wind it tightly around the wire of the structure six times, thread on a bead, make another six turns, thread on another bead, and so on.

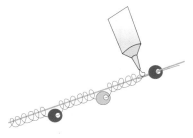

5 When you come to the end of the medium wire, apply a little glue before threading your final bead on to both wires. Bend and shape each of the six beaded wires into a spiral.

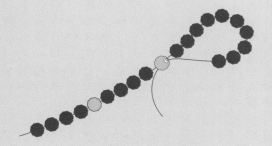

HOOK

6 Cut a 30cm (12in) length of thin purple wire. Wind it tightly around the base of one of the spirals. Thread on 7cm (2¾in) of beads, alternating the colours as you go, and make a loop by threading the wire back through one of the beads. Thread on another 7cm (2¾in) of beads and wind the purple wire to the base of the opposite spiral.

PENDANTS

7 Make six pendants to hang from the base spokes of the chandelier and six to hang from the spirals. Use two small red faceted beads for the lower pendants and three small red faceted beads for the upper pendants. Take the wire through a large faceted bead and a small pink bead then back over the small pink bead and wrap firmly to secure (see diagram above). Attach them to the chandelier by winding the wire twice around each spiral and the base of the

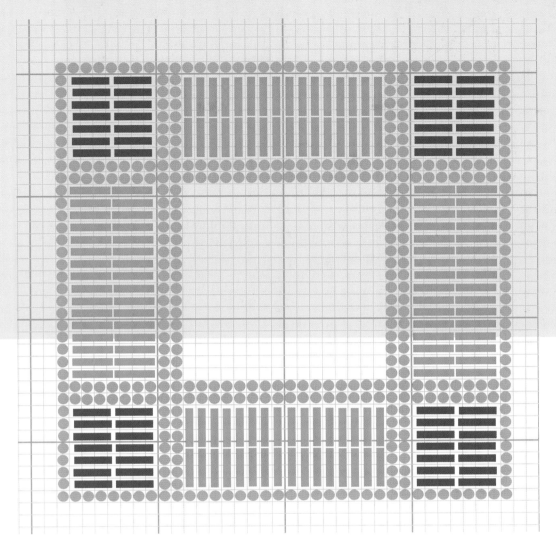

EMBROIDERED PHOTO FRAME (SEE PAGE 8)

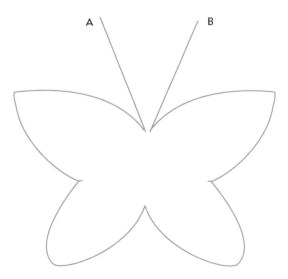

BUTTERFLY TUMBLERS (SEE PAGE 16)

Index